Ocean Animals
DOLPHINS

By Walter LaPlante

Please visit our website, www.garethstevens.com. For a free color catalog of all our high-quality books, call toll free 1-800-542-2595 or fax 1-877-542-2596.

Library of Congress Cataloging-in-Publication Data

Names: LaPlante, Walter, author.
Title: Dolphins / Walter LaPlante.
Description: New York : Gareth Stevens Publishing, [2020] | Series: Ocean animals
Identifiers: LCCN 2019010482| ISBN 9781538244531 (paperback) | ISBN 9781538244555 (library bound) | ISBN 9781538244548 (6 pack)
Subjects: LCSH: Dolphins–Juvenile literature.
Classification: LCC QL737.C432 L36 2020 | DDC 599.53–dc23
LC record available at https://lccn.loc.gov/2019010482

First Edition

Published in 2020 by
Gareth Stevens Publishing
111 East 14th Street, Suite 349
New York, NY 10003

Copyright © 2020 Gareth Stevens Publishing

Designer: Katelyn E. Reynolds
Editor: Kristen Rajczak Nelson

Photo credits: Cover, p. 1 FLICKETTI/Shutterstock.com; p. 5 Willyam Bradberry/Shutterstock.com; p. 7 juanmanuelbuceo/Shutterstock.com; p. 9 Chase Dekker/Shutterstock.com; pp. 11, 24 (fin) COULANGES/Shutterstock.com; pp. 13, 24 (tail) dean bertoncelj/Shutterstock.com; p. 15 Paul Vinten/Shutterstock.com; p. 17 wildestanimal/Shutterstock.com; pp. 19, 21 vkilikov/Shutterstock.com; p. 23 oneinchpunch/Shutterstock.com.

All rights reserved. No part of this book may be reproduced in any form without permission in writing from the publisher, except by a reviewer.

Printed in the United States of America

Some of the images in this book illustrate individuals who are models. The depictions do not imply actual situations or events.

CPSIA compliance information: Batch #CW20GS: For further information contact Gareth Stevens, New York, New York at 1-800-542-2595.

Contents

Ocean Living 4

All About Their Body 8

Family Life 14

See One! 22

Words to Know 24

Index 24

Dolphins live in the ocean!

Some live
in warm water.
Some live
in colder water!

They are gray.
Their backs are
a darker gray.

They have three fins.

They have a tail.
It helps them swim fast!

Dolphins live
in big groups.

They catch fish together.

They have one baby at a time.

Babies stay
with their mother
for years.

You might see one at the zoo!

Words to Know

fins

tail

Index

babies 18, 20

color 8

food 16